THE STORY OF
COCA-COLA

L O N N I E   B E L L

Published by Smart Apple Media
1980 Lookout Drive, North Mankato, Minnesota 56003

Photography by Corbis (AFP, Bettmann, Macduff Everton, Jacques Langevin,
Wally McNamee, Minnesota Historical Society, Richard T. Nowitz, Roger Ressmeyer,
Hersch Steven/Sygma, Nik Wheeler), Richard Cummins, Fred R. Hight, Sally McCrae
Kuyper, Bill Morgenstern, PR News Foto, Time Life Pictures/Getty Images, (Robin
Moyer, Ted Thai, Time Inc., Hank Walker), D. Jeanene Tiner, Unicorn Stock Photos
(Tommy Dodson, Mark Gibson, Jean Higgins, Andre Jenny)

Library of Congress Cataloging-in-Publication Data
Bell, Lonnie.
The story of Coca-Cola / by Lonnie Bell.
p. cm. — (Built for success)
Summary: Discusses the founding and development of Coca-Cola,
which calls itself "the world's soft drink."
Includes bibliographical references.
ISBN 1-58340-292-6
1. Coca-Cola Company—History—Juvenile literature. 2. Soft drink
industry—United States—History—Juvenile literature. [1. Coca-Cola
Company—History.] I. Title. II. Series.
HD9349.S634 C5333 2003
338.7'66362'0973—dc21
2002036567

2 4 6 8 9 7 5 3

THE STORY OF

COCA-COLA

Table of Contents

The Birth of Coca-Cola

Coca-Cola calls itself "the world's soft drink" for a good reason. People in nearly 200 countries drink more than one billion eight-ounce (237 ml) servings of Coca-Cola products every day. So much Coke has been produced since the first batch in 1886 that if a person put it all into eight-ounce (237 ml) bottles and stacked them up, they would tower 370 miles (595 km). That's 67 times taller than Mount Everest, the tallest mountain in the world! Coca-Cola didn't become the number one soft drink overnight, of course. It started more than 100 years ago with a man named John Pemberton.

Today Coke is a **carbonated** soft drink, but when it was first created it had no bubbles at all. Dr. John Pemberton, a **pharmacist** from Atlanta, Georgia, developed the formula for Coca-Cola syrup in a three-legged brass pot. The two chief ingredients were **extracts** of the coca plant (which Coca-Cola no longer contains) and the kola nut. Pemberton, who made **tonics** for illnesses and health problems, may have been working on a headache cure when he created the syrup that would one day become Coca-Cola.

Pemberton liked the way his new tonic tasted, and he decided to take it to Jacobs' Pharmacy, the largest pharmacy in Atlanta. Drugstores at the time had soda fountains where customers enjoyed drinks and other refreshments. Pemberton asked the manager, Willis Venable, to mix his tonic with water and sell it at the soda fountain as a tonic for headaches and tiredness. Venable agreed to sell it for five cents a glass.

Pemberton's partner and bookkeeper, Frank Robinson, suggested the name "Coca-Cola" for the drink because he thought the two capital Cs would look good in advertise-

Sodas contained syrup, carbonated water, and ice cream

ments. He drew the letters in the same graceful style of print used today. A few weeks after Jacobs' Pharmacy began selling Coca-Cola, Pemberton and Robinson ran the first advertisement for the product in the *Atlanta Daily Journal*. The ad claimed Coca-Cola was "Delicious! Refreshing! Exhilarating! Invigorating!" "Delicious and Refreshing" became the first official **slogan** used by Coca-Cola.

Later that same year, someone accidentally added carbonated water instead of plain water to the Coke syrup. Customers who tried the new bubbly drink liked it better, and it has been served as a carbonated drink ever since.

Customers liked Coca-Cola, but it was not an instant success. Pemberton sold only 25 gallons (95 l) of syrup the first year and received about $50 for his trouble. He still believed in his tonic, but his health was failing, and he didn't have the strength or money to promote Coca-Cola properly.

Popular Coke Slogans

1886	Delicious and Refreshing
1906	The Great National Temperance
1917	Three Million a Day
1927	Around the Corner from Everywhere
1929	The Pause that Refreshes
1942	The Only Thing Like Coca-Cola is Coca-Cola Itself. It's the Real Thing!
1952	What You Want Is a Coke
1963	Things Go Better with Coke
1969	It's the Real Thing
1979	Have a Coke and a Smile
1982	Coke Is It!
1988	You Can't Beat the Feeling
1990	Can't Beat the Real Thing
1993	Always Coca-Cola
2000	Coca-Cola. Enjoy!
2001	Life Tastes Good
2002	Reward your Curiosity (Vanilla Coke slogan)
2003	Coca-Cola . . . Real

Dr. Pemberton had been a Confederate lieutenant general

In 1891, a man named Asa Candler bought Coca-Cola from Pemberton for $2,300. Candler was interested in the product because he suffered from headaches. He had heard that the Coca-Cola tonic could help. When he tried it, he found that it did, in fact, ease his headaches. After buying the Coca-Cola Company, Candler even advertised the drink as "The Wonderful Nerve and Brain Tonic."

Believing that advertising would boost the sales of his new soft drink, Candler sent coupons for free drinks to pharmacies that sold his syrup. He put the Coca-Cola name on

Early ads featured glamorous women enjoying Coca-Cola

calendars, coasters, posters, clocks, and other items. Within four years, soda fountains in every state and territory of the United States sold Coke syrup.

Candler registered the name "Coca-Cola" with the U.S. Patent Office as an official **trademark** in 1893. He wanted customers to call the drink by the original name, even though people were already calling it by a new nickname, Coke. Eventually, in 1945, the Coca-Cola Company also registered the name "Coke" as a trademark.

Asa Candler was an Atlanta doctor and pharmacist

Taking Coca-Cola Home

In the beginning, Coca-Cola was sold only as a syrup that had to be mixed with water at soda fountains. Mr. Candler had no interest in putting the drink in bottles because bottling was a slow and awkward task at the time. Bottles were sealed with a cork and wire hook. When opened, the cork went down into the bottle and stayed there. This made cleaning and refilling bottles difficult and time-consuming. The bottles also tended to explode, which could be dangerous and costly.

One soda fountain owner, Joseph Biedenharn, thought bottling the popular drink made sense. He wanted to sell Coke to people who lived outside U.S. cities where there were no soda fountains. In 1894, he set up a bottling machine in his store and became the first person to bottle Coke.

In 1899, two businessmen from Tennessee, Benjamin Thomas and Joseph Whitehead, paid Candler one dollar for the right to bottle and sell Coca-Cola throughout the U.S. Since setting up bottling plants was expensive, they came up with the idea of **independent bottlers**. They signed **contracts** with people who wanted to bottle Coke. The independent bot-

The invention of the bottlecap in 1892 changed bottling

tlers provided the employees, factories, bottles, and machinery. The Coca-Cola Company provided the Coca-Cola syrup and helped the bottlers with training and advertising. Using this bottling method, Coca-Cola could sell its soft drink across the country—and eventually around the would.

There were many other soda fountain drinks during the late 1880s and early 1900s when Coke got its start. Most of them had fruity flavors, such as orange, lemon, and strawberry. Once Coca-Cola became popular, other soft-drink companies naturally wanted to make similar beverages. Some even copied

A 1950 *Time* magazine cover depicted Coke's global appeal

the style of lettering Coca-Cola used. Even Dr. Pemberton, the man who made the original batch of Coca-Cola, began creating new tonics and selling them. There were an estimated 150 brands trying to copy Coke. Among the competitors were King Cola, Cola Ree, Gay-Ola, Cold Cola, and Candy Cola.

Coca-Cola did not want to lose its customers to imitators, so company officials decided to find a way to make Coca-Cola stand out. At that time, all soft-drink bottles had straight sides. In 1915, Coke bottlers hired the Root Glass Company to design the unique, curved-glass Coca-Cola bottle.

There are two stories about how the glass company got the idea for the design. One legend says that the shape was similar to a hobble skirt—a long, tight skirt in fashion at the time. The other explains that the company was trying to mimic the shape of a coca bean. Either way, the curved bottle was different enough from other bottles that Coca-Cola was able to register it as a trademark. In 1929, after the curved bottle proved successful, Coke designed a special bell-shaped fountain glass for serving the soft drink.

Early vending machines had built-in bottle openers

New Look, New Ideas

In 1919, Mr. Candler sold his business to a banker named Ernest Woodruff for $25 million. Four years later, Mr. Woodruff's son, Robert Winship Woodruff, was elected president and took over the company's leadership. The younger Woodruff continued to be actively involved in the company for the next 60 years.

Robert Woodruff believed in quality. He started a training program for soda fountain operators to make sure they served the drink correctly. He took advantage of new **technology** to help boost sales of Coca-Cola. In the early 1920s, for example, Coke was sold from the first soft-drink vending machines. Coke bottles were kept cooled in chests of crushed ice. People dropped coins in a cash box or paid a clerk before taking a Coke. In later vending machine models, bottles hung from a metal rack inside the chest. Customers inserted a coin into a coin slot, slid a Coke bottle to the end of the rack, and lifted it out. The ice chests allowed people to buy Coca-Cola in offices, factories, and businesses. Visitors to the 1933 Chicago World's Fair were surprised by another new invention:

the automatic fountain dispenser. Instead of mixing carbonated water with syrup, Coke was now premixed and served cold from a single dispenser.

Americans loved Coke, but it was sold in only five countries outside of the United States when Mr. Woodruff bought the business. In 1928, the Coca-Cola Company discovered a clever way to reach people from nearly every country in the world. Coca-Cola became the first soft drink served at the Olympic Games. The company shipped 1,000 cases of Coke to the 1928 Summer Olympics in Amsterdam. Vendors

Robert Woodruff was highly respected by his employees

Above, a billboard in three languages;
below, Coca-Cola is sold in China

wearing clothes with the Coca-Cola name sold cold drinks to about 40,000 spectators in the stadium. Others sold Coke outside the stadium at small stands called winkles.

By the time the United States entered World War II in the 1940s, Coca-Cola was bottled in 44 countries—including some that were at war with the United States. During the war, Woodruff's goal was to provide every man and woman in uniform with Coke—no matter where they were stationed. Coca-Cola opened 64 plants overseas during the war. Not only did this familiar drink from home lift the spirits of American troops, it also gave the residents of other countries a chance to try Coca-Cola for the first time.

While the taste of Coca-Cola stayed the same throughout the years, the containers changed with the times. For 40 years, Coke was sold at soda fountains in the traditional curved bottles and bell-shaped glasses. In the 1950s, Coke introduced a choice of bottles in 10-, 12-, and 26-ounce (296, 355, and 769 ml) sizes. The larger bottles were an instant hit. Metal cans came on the scene in the 1960s and quickly became the most convenient and popular packaging

for soft drinks. In 1978, Coca-Cola made history when it introduced the first plastic PET (polyethylene terphthalate) bottle, which is now used by most soft-drink bottlers. When **consumers** grew concerned about pollution, Coke responded by encouraging people to **recycle** cans and bottles.

In 1960, Coca-Cola added its first new product line in the United States, Fanta. Fanta products, which come in a variety of fruit flavors such as orange and grape, had been sold by Coke bottlers in other countries for many years. It still ranks as one of the world's top five soft drinks.

Fanta is popular in Nepal and other Asian countries

Coke added Sprite to its lineup a year later. The name "Sprite" came from an earlier advertisement for Coca-Cola. In the 1940s, Coke had used a little man with a big smile in its ads. He had white hair and wore a bottle cap for a hat. Eventually he became known as the Sprite Boy, after elf-like creatures called sprites that feature in many folk tales. When Coca-Cola developed its citrus-flavored drink, company leaders thought the short, spunky name of the Sprite Boy fit the product well. Another drink company was using the name, but Coke was able to buy the rights back.

The Sprite Boy was created by artist Haddon Sundblom

Tab, Coke's first low-calorie drink, was introduced in 1963. In 1982, the company introduced diet Coke, or Coca-Cola light, as it is known in some countries. Diet Coke quickly became the most popular low-calorie drink in the world. While diet Coke sales are much higher than sales of Tab, the Coca-Cola Company still produces a small quantity of Tab to satisfy its small, but loyal, following. Coke purchased the Minute Maid Company, producer of juice products, in 1960 and introduced a new line of Minute Maid soft drinks to the United States in 1987.

In 2001, recognizing that consumers often enjoyed diet Coke with a slice of lemon, the company introduced diet Coke with lemon flavor added in North America. A year later, Coca-Cola introduced Vanilla Coke. The new flavor is based on a simple recipe that customers have used for years—vanilla flavoring added to Coke. It was the first major flavor extension of the Coca-Cola Classic line in 16 years. Soon after, the company launched diet Vanilla Coke.

Coca-Cola Products

1886	Coca-Cola
1960	Fanta
1961	Sprite
1963	Tab
1966	Fresca
1972	Mr. Pibb
1979	Mello Yello
1982	Diet Coke
1983	Caffeine-free Coke products
1985	Cherry Coke, new Coke, Minute Maid Orange Soda
1992	Powerade
1994	Fruitopia
1997	Surge
2001	Diet Coke with lemon
2002	Vanilla Coke, diet Vanilla Coke, Nestle's Choglit milk-based drink

Minute Maid introduced Fruitopia soft drinks in 1994

Marketing Coca-Cola

Coca-Cola owes some of its success to the clever way the company markets its soft drinks. To **market** a product means to come up with a plan that will convince consumers to buy it. Coca-Cola followed up on Mr. Candler's early interest in advertising and continued to look for interesting ways to spread the word about its products. After Coke began to be bottled and sold nationwide, the Coca-Cola Company hired famous artists such as Norman Rockwell to paint heart-warming images of families enjoying Coca-Cola. It used the artwork in magazine and newspaper ads, calendars, and posters.

The company also continued to add catchy new slogans to its early trademark, "Delicious and Refreshing." "It's the Real Thing," was first used in the 1940s and was reintroduced in the late 1960s. "Coke Is It!" was the choice for the 1980s. As radio and television became increasingly commonplace in homes worldwide, the company expanded these slogans into jingles, songs written for an advertising campaign. The jingles were recorded by well-known signing groups of the time, such as the Supremes and Jan and Dean in the

1960s. One of the company's most popular jingles was "Things Go Better With Coke" from the 1960s, which was recorded by more than 60 different singers and musical groups.

Pairing up products with celebrities is a common way to advertise today, but Coca-Cola combined famous faces with its products as early as 1950. Coke sponsored its first television program, *The Edgar Bergan and Charlie McCarthy Show*, that year. Edgar Bergan was an actor and ventriloquist, and Charlie was his sidekick dummy. Since then, Coke has used many movie actors, singers, and sports figures to pro-

Edgar Bergan and Charlie McCarthy were a hit on Coke's TV show

Joe Greene was the star of a popular Coke commercial

mote its drinks. In the 1970s, Coke used its slogan "Have a Coke and a Smile" as the theme for one of the best-loved television commercials of the decade. The commercial featured a young boy who shared a cold Coke with Pittsburgh Steelers tackle "Mean" Joe Greene during a professional football game. In the end, Mr. Greene tossed the boy his jersey as a souvenir and gave him a smile.

In the mid-1980s, Coca-Cola still produced the top-selling soft drink, but Pepsi-Cola was becoming more and more popular. Pepsi ran two successful **ad campaigns**. The "Pepsi Generation" ads claimed that Pepsi was the drink for young, hip consumers. The ads worked. Pepsi sales climbed, and the so-called "cola wars" began.

The second Pepsi campaign, "The Pepsi Challenge," hit Coke even harder. Pepsi began airing television commercials with ordinary people taking the Pepsi Challenge by tasting Pepsi and Coca-Cola side by side without knowing which was which. In the ads, many tasters who said they were Coke drinkers chose Pepsi over Coke in the blind taste test. This made Coca-Cola nervous.

This Coca-Cola bottling factory is fancifully designed

The Coca-Cola Company studied the problem and decided that people's tastes must be changing. Company **executives** believed people wanted a soft drink that tasted more like Pepsi, which was lighter and sweeter than Coke. The Coca-Cola Company did something no one thought it would ever do: it announced a plan to get rid of the 99-year-old Coke formula and introduce a sweeter, softer Coke. Everyone, including Pepsi, was surprised. Many loyal Coke drinkers were angry and refused to drink new Coke, as it was called. During this period, Pepsi sales increased, and it briefly became the number one soft drink.

After letters and phone calls poured in asking for the old Coke, the Coca-Cola Company announced the return of the original formula with a new name—Coca-Cola classic. Some Coke drinkers believe the company didn't return to the exact formula it used before, but no one really knows for sure, since the formula has been a well-kept secret from the beginning. Dropping the traditional Coke formula was clearly a mistake, but the company learned something. It discovered how loyal Coke drinkers were.

In 2000, serious problems in Europe threatened that loyalty. It was believed that **contaminated** Coca-Cola products were making people sick. Authorities discovered that Coca-Cola products had an "off taste" and bad smell. It turned out that the problems were caused by poor quality carbonation at local bottling plants. The beverages were not toxic, but Coca-Cola's reputation suffered. The company fixed the problems and began working to regain customer trust.

Over the next two years, Coca-Cola developed marketing programs to rebuild trust and connect with its cus-

Many Coke lovers organized protests against new Coke

tomers. The company worked hard to find out what customers in different countries wanted. It then created products based on what customers asked for. Computer-savvy teens throughout Great Britain, for instance, participated in the "Real Coke Rush," an online auction. Coca-Cola ring pulls and labels were used to purchase prizes on the Internet. The program won 10 awards for excellence. In Chile, parents said they wanted healthier drinks, so Coca-Cola introduced Bibo, a brand of snack drinks fortified with vitamins. Burn, a high-energy drink, was developed for young people in Australia who wanted something to drink on their nights out. When the company introduced a health drink called Qoo, it quickly became the number-one selling juice in Japan.

Sometimes, however, trust isn't built with a marketing plan. It comes straight from the heart. That was certainly the case when on September 11, 2001, thousands of Coca-Cola bottling partners used their trucks and distribution centers to deliver whatever was needed to help people in New York City and Washington, D.C., after terrorists attacked the World Trade Center and the Pentagon.

Coca-Cola was affected by the September 11 attacks

The World's Favorite Soft Drink

Many Coke fans enjoy collecting Coca-Cola items. Any object that bears the name of Coca-Cola products is considered a collectible. Some early Coke items may be worth a good deal of money, but not all collectibles are antiques. People can find all types of Coke collectibles, from ceiling fans and ballpoint pens to toys and T-shirts. The Coca-Cola Company doesn't actually make all these things. Manufacturers pay the company a fee for a **license** to use the Coca-Cola name.

One collectible that continues to delight Coke fans of all ages is the white polar bear Coke used in its 1990s television commercials with the slogan, "Always Coca-Cola." The bear is still sold as a stuffed animal and makes appearances on other items, particularly in the winter.

Christmas ornaments and holiday items have long been favorite Coke collectibles. In 1931, an artist named Haddon Sundblom was hired to paint Santa Claus for Coca-Cola ads. Before his drawings, there were many versions of what Santa Claus looked like—some artists drew him as a jolly elf; others pictured him as tall and thin. Sundblom's vision of Santa as the

Above, a Coca-Cola delivery truck; left, a mule delivers
Coke in Italy; right, cans of Coca-Cola for the troops

chubby, cheery man with a great white beard and round, red cheeks is how Americans still think of Santa Claus today.

The World of Coca-Cola, a three-story pavilion, opened in Atlanta, Georgia, in 1990. This museum celebrates the history of Coca-Cola and its products with a series of exhibits displaying more than 1,000 pieces of Coke **memorabilia**. Visitors can learn about the history of the company and the soft-drink bottling industry or view 10-minute films that highlight famous Coke television commercials from the past. On display are soda fountain equipment and early bottling machines. As visitors exit the museum, they can sample different Coca-Cola products, including exotic drinks that Coke bottlers sell in other countries, such as Maaza, a noncarbonat-

Annual Consumption of Coca-Cola Products*	
Region	8-oz. (237 ml) servings per person
Worldwide	70
North America**	398
United States	419
Latin America	205
Argentina	236
Brazil	144
Chile	336
Mexico	462
Europe, Eurasia, & Middle East	72
Eurasia	39
France	110
Germany	193
Great Britain	193
Italy	104
Middle East	17
Spain	264
Asia	23
Australia	303
China	9
Japan	168
Korea	71
Phillippines	159
Africa	34
North & West Africa	26
Southern & East Africa	44

Source: The Coca-Cola Company 2001
*Excludes products distributed by the Minute Maid Company.
**Includes United States, Canada, Puerto Rico, and Minute Maid products.

ed, mango-flavored drink from India, and Lift, a lemon-lime beverage from Australia. Coca-Cola has also opened two stores, in Las Vegas and New York City.

Coca-Cola has come a long way since Mr. Pemberton's discovery more than 100 years ago. The Coca-Cola Company is the largest beverage company in the world, with plants in nearly 200 countries bottling and distributing the drink. Pemberton and Candler would be delighted to learn that Coca-Cola continues to be the most popular fountain drink around.

According to the Coca-Cola Company, it took 22 years to sell its first one billion servings of Coke products. By the late 1990s, it was selling one billion servings of its soft drinks in a single day. To stay on top in the future, Coca-Cola must continue to grow, selling more Coke products in both the United States and in foreign countries. The company must also come up with fresh ideas to keep consumers happy.

Selling new products to other countries can be a challenge. People from other countries may speak different languages and have different tastes than people in the United

Coca-Cola opened a store on "the Strip" in Las Vegas

States. Companies such as Coca-Cola must find out which products appeal to the residents of a particular country or they must create new products that they may like even better. In Japan, for example, Coca-Cola bottlers sell the Georgia Coffee line along with Coke, while flavored teas are popular with Chinese consumers. Reaching new Coke drinkers requires special advertising suited to each country, so Coca-Cola uses many different agencies to design commercials and advertisements for radio, television, newspapers, magazines, and billboards around the world.

Coca-Cola sponsors this bus stop in China

As Coca-Cola moves into the 21st century, it continues to create new products that people love. The company is finding fresh ways to build trust with consumers and market products to thirsty people everywhere. Someone chooses a Coca-Cola—diet or light or classic, with cherry or lemon or vanilla, with or without caffeine—nearly every minute of every day. Even so, there are still people in the world who have never had their first sip of Coke. The Coca-Cola Company plans to change that. Perhaps Coca-Cola will one day be the most popular drink in every country and truly become "the world's soft drink."

The Coca-Cola Foundation

The Coca-Cola Company is committed to giving something back to communities in the United States and other nations. In 1984, the company started the Coca-Cola Foundation to help fund education programs around the world. During the 1990s, it contributed $100 million to education. The foundation supports the Pipeline Program, aimed at keeping children from dropping out of school. The Coca-Cola Foundation also funds global art and business-management education programs and offers a wide range of college scholarships.

An African family drinks Coke at the 1996 Olympics

1886   Dr. John Pemberton formulates Coca-Cola.

1891   Asa Candler buys the Coca-Cola formula for $2,300.

1893   Candler registers "Coca-Cola" as a trademark.

1899   Candler grants Benjamin Thomas and Joseph Whitehead the right to bottle Coke.

1915   The Root Glass Company designs a unique, curved bottle for Coca-Cola.

1919   Ernest Woodruff buys the Coca-Cola Company for $25 million.

1923   Robert Woodruff is elected president of the Coca-Cola Company.

1928   Coke is first sold at the Olympic Games.

1929   The Coca-Cola Company introduces its famous bell-shaped glasses.

1945   "Coke" becomes a registered trademark.

1960   The Coca-Cola Company adds its first new product line in the U.S., Fanta.

1985   The cola wars cause the Coca-Cola Company to change its formula and introduce new Coke. After Coke drinkers complain, the original formula is reintroduced with a new name: Coca-Cola classic.

1985 The Coca-Cola Company introduces a new line of Minute Maid juice drinks.

1990 The World of Coca-Cola opens in Atlanta, Georgia.

1996 Coca-Cola signs a unique contract to sponsor the Olympic Games through 2008.

1997 Coca-Cola introduces Surge, a citrus soda packed with caffeine and sugar.

2001 The Coca-Cola Company develops reading programs in local communities as a marketing partner with Warner Brothers Pictures. The programs build on interest in reading inspired by *Harry Potter* books and movies.

2001 Growth in sales of bottled water is second only to carbonated soft drinks. Coca-Cola's Dasani becomes the nation's fastest-growing water brand.

2002 Coca-Cola introduces Vanilla Coke, the first major line extension of the Coca-Cola trademark since 1985.

GLOSSARY

ad campaigns Planned series of ads with a common theme.

carbonated Made bubbly using carbon dioxide.

consumers People who buy and consume, or use, a product or a service.

contaminated Made unfit for use by mixture with undesirable or unwholesome elements.

contracts Written agreements made between two parties in which each promises to meet certain obligations.

executives A company's leaders, such as its president and top managers. Executives make important decisions for a company.

extracts Concentrated substances that are extracted, or taken out of, their sources, such as plants or fruit. An extract has a stronger flavor and smell than its source.

independent bottlers People who pay for a license to establish a bottling plant. Soft-drink companies give independent bottlers assistance with advertising and training and provide supplies and ingredients (such as syrup) to make their products.

license Permission to use a company name, slogan, or image, granted by the copyright owner.

market To promote or advertise a product to consumers.

memorabilia Objects that are reminders of the past.

pharmacist A person who prepares and distributes medicines.

recycle To process a used material (such as plastic, aluminum, or glass) so that it can be used again.

slogan A short, attention-getting phrase used in advertising.

technology Science that is used to provide something people need or want.

tonics Mixtures designed to refresh and restore people's energy.

trademark A symbol or name that belongs legally and exclusively to one company. It may also refer to something that is unique about a company.

Atlanta's Coca-Cola museum is an impressive sight

INDEX

INDEX

Books

Beyer, Chris H. *Coca-Cola Girls: an Advertising Art History*. Portland, Ore.: Collectors Press, 2001.

Pendergrast, Mark. *For God, Country and Coca-Cola: The Definitive History of the Great American Soft Drink and the Company that Makes It*. Macon, Ga.: Mercer University Press, 2000.

Zubrowski, Bernie. *Soda Science: Designing and Testing Soft Drinks*. New York: William Morrow & Co., 1997.

Web Sites

The Coca-Cola Company's official Web site
http://www.cocacola.com

World of Coca-Cola, Atlanta
http://www.woccAtlanta.com

The official Web site of the Coca-Cola Collectors
http://cocacolaclub.org

Highlights in the History of Coca-Cola Television Advertising
http://memory.loc.gov/ammem/ccmphtml/colahist.html